YOUR DAUGHTER HAS BEEN DIAGNOSED
WITH RETT SYNDROME
Copyright 2005, Kim Isaac Greenblatt.

Published in West Hills, California, USA.
ISBN-10 0-9777282-0-X
ISBN-13 978-0-9777282-0-6

Library of Congress Control Number:
2006900176

Dedicated to my wife, Sharren, my son, Jacob and of course, my lovely daughter, Arianna .

TABLE OF CONTENTS

iv

INTRODUCTION

Welcome! You've come to this book from one of the following perspectives:

1. You are a parent who has a daughter who has stopped talking, walking, communicating, or has not walked, talked etc and the medical community is ready to label her with a generic "autistic" label. Your daughter (or in rare cases your son) may wring her (or his) hands a lot? Maybe there has been deterioration or zero development in communication or body movement? Maybe your child is 2 years old and not developing "age appropriately"?

First – slow down and take a breath. You are NOT alone. A lot of us have been through the path before you and we are here to help! Keep reading....

2.   You are the friend or loved one of somebody who has received a diagnosis of Rett's Syndrome.

3.   You are a medical, educational or social professional seeking more information about Rett Syndrome.

If you are here from the second or third points of view, this book will start you on the path to understanding what is going on with the angel that you are looking at who has Rett's Syndrome.

If you are here from the first point of view we may be able to help you and offer some guide posts to illuminate your path in trying to figure out what is going on and what to do!

First, if you haven't already done it – find a doctor who can write you a prescription for a test for MECP2 (methyl-CpG-binding protein-2).   It is an enzyme which, when mutated, results in RTT (Rett syndrome).

The test is a blood test and costs maybe a few hundred dollars tops. It may be covered by your insurance plan. It will result in you getting a diagnosis with a 99.9% certainty that your daughter (or in very rare cases) your son has Rett's Syndrome. If your child doesn't test positive for Rett's Syndrome that is not to say that the child doesn't have it – it just means that your child is outside the normal spectrum for Rett's Syndrome. Tests are able to confirm a clinical diagnosis in up to 80% of the cases . The other 20% are described as having "atypical" or "variant" Rett Syndrome.

Next, keep reading this book. I am the proud father of a daughter with Rett's Syndrome and have tackled (and continue to tackle) a lot of the issues that are out there that you are concerned about. When my wife, Sharren, and I received our diagnosis about Rett Syndrome for our daughter, Arianna, we had nothing to place it in perspective with. We were handed a photocopy of a document printed in a manual from the 1960's that had a prognosis of early death! We received that on Arianna's 3rd birthday and needless to say were depressed and in tears.

But you have this book – hooray! It shouldn't be that way for you!

Hopefully the book will be able to answer some questions you have and that in turn will lead to more questions which will help you care for your daughter, cope with your situation and find love, life and laughter with some of the stress, fear and depression that you may be feeling.

Let's see what we can do to start improving everybody's quality of life!

Kim Greenblatt
November 7, 2005
West Hills, California

CHAPTER 1

WHAT IS RETT'S SYNDROME?

Rett Syndrome is a genetic disease named after the person who first described it, Andreas Rett, an Austrian pediatrician in 1966. The disease is very unusual because generally ONLY girls have it. It is an X-linked dominant disorder that is lethal in males. In other words, if a male has the Rett syndrome gene (the symbol for that is RTT), the male generally dies before birth. If a female receives the Rett Syndrome gene, she gets Rett Syndrome. In 1999, the gene that causes Rett Syndrome was discovered and can be tested for.

As of the printing of this book (2006), in at least 80% of the cases of Rett Syndrome, the disease appears to be passed as a genetic mutation in the male sperm. Scientists are trying to research why this is happening. The frequency of Rett Syndrome is about 1 in 15,000 girls. Subsequent editions of this book will have more information as it develops!

Symptoms of Rett Syndrome are as follows:

1.   Wringing of the hands.

2.   Reduced or loss of muscle tone (The medical term for that is hypotonia).

3.   Seizures.

4.   Teepee folding of hands.

5.   Diminished ability to express feelings and autistic behavior.

6.   Loss of speech.

7.   Avoidance of eye contact.

8.   Gait (walking or standing) abnormalities.

9.   Lag in brain and head growth.

The good news is that the majority of girls with Rett Syndrome can be expected to reach adulthood and live at least into their 40s and 50s. As more information gets accumulated, more information on life expectancy can be extrapolated.

The severity of the symptoms varies from individual to individual. Some girls have symptoms from birth. Arianna, our daughter, did not crawl and rolled or dragged herself. Some Rett girls do not walk at all.

The scientific reasoning for this is because girls (females) have two copies of the X chromosome. Females only need one set for genetic information. The other "extra" X chromosome is turned off. The process is called *X inactivation.* This process occurs randomly so that each cell is left with one active X chromosome. The severity of Rett syndrome in girls is in part a function of the percentage of cells with a normal copy of the MECP2 gene after X inactivation takes place. In other words, if X inactivation turns off the X chromosome that is carrying the defective gene in a large proportion of cells, the symptoms will be mild. If a greater percentage of cells have the X chromosome with the normal MECP2 gene turned off, earlier and more severe symptoms occur. Clear as mud, isn't it?

At the present time, there is no cure for Rett Syndrome. All the work is in management of the symptoms. Examples of symptom support (which will vary from girl to girl) are:

Seizure control. This was a big deal for Arianna.

Medicines to control breathing or motor difficulties.

Prevention and correction of scoliosis and heart problems. This is an issue for a lot of Rett children.

Occupational therapy for dressing, feeding, arts, hobbies.

Any therapy that can prolong mobility such as physiotherapy, hydrotherapy, equestrian therapy.

Items like braces and splints to prevent scoliosis and direct hand and leg movements.

Academic, vocational, social and support services to allow integration into society.

Just as a heads-up, if you have a diagnosis of autism and are already receiving therapies you may lose services by changing it to a Rett Syndrome diagnosis. Be aware of that and act accordingly.

RETT SYNDROME STAGES

Rett's Syndrome is broken down into "stages". While these stages may not match what other books or references talk about, the following stages are presented generic enough to cover what happens when a girl develops Rett's.

Stage 1 -From 6 months to 18 months, the girl develops normally.

Stage 2 –There is stagnation and deterioration as higher brain functions stop working.

There is loss of speech, autistic behavior, hand-wringing, loss of purposeful use of the hands, wobbliness while standing, hyperventilation, seizures (sometimes) and the body, specifically the head, does not appear to grow. When the head does not grow it is called, microcephaly or small head.

Stage 3 –Things appear to be stable. There may be seizures, spastic papparesis which means paralysis and spasticity of the legs.

Rett girls may also stop growing and be short and have microcephaly.

As the Rett girls get older, they are at risk for heart conduction problems.

Okay, now that I have scared you with some general information and statistics, let's look at this from some practical points of view.

The girls are still our daughters. Nothing has changed them from before you got (or are getting your diagnosis). All this means is that you know what you are dealing with. When my wife, Sharren, and I received our diagnosis, we were upset but that did not change our feelings for Arianna. We had suffered other things in our past (that is for another book!) and practically, other than somebody giving Arianna a label, it didn't change Arianna one bit!

There is no need for incriminations. As stated previously, at this point, nobody knows what is causing the mutation at this time. Nobody.

In some cases – the blame game starts.

First and foremost – forgive yourself because if you are already blaming yourself you are doing your daughter an injustice. As the saying goes, you also need to forgive yourself before you can forgive others.

The three emotion trifecta (a trifecta is a bet where you pick the three winners of a race or contest) that we went through as parents were denial, fear and anger (with denial winning first place and fear and anger jockeying for second and third place).

Comments Sharren and I had were, "Oh my God, this can't be happening to me."

"Doctor, you are wrong. This can't be the problem. No, no, nooooooo."

Everybody can react this way. It is a normal reaction. It then blends quickly into anger or fear with the emotions directed to in no particular order, your spouse, yourself, your children, medical personnel who are trying to help, social service people, well-meaning relatives and sometimes anybody who looks at you cross-eyed.

The only reason Sharren and I did not go through this as deeply with Arianna was because we went through this in another situation which if you have already suffered enough in life and learnt your lesson, you can move on to learn other lessons. If you are experiencing any of the emotions I talked about – that is normal. Again, you are not alone!!

That reminds me of the "NOT" items.

Even though editors and writers say not to emphasis negatives or "nots" I felt it was important that I include a "NOT" list. You will see why in a moment.

It is NOT dad's fault, it is NOT mom's fault.

Anger will have you blaming everybody. That is a normal overwhelming emotion but it has no bearing on genetics. It is very frustrating to deal with. Anger is an intense emotion. You really want to blame somebody to try and make yourself feel better!

Physical exercise and working a hobby can help alleviate anger. I spend a lot of time with my family as well as working. Don't you wish sometimes that you didn't have to work for a living? Have you ever come home from work tired and mad? I would and even if I wouldn't let the anger out it would boil and boil. I found a great release in physical exercise.

I try to walk 2 miles a day as well as make individual "me" time for hobbies like making my own homemade soda and playing videogames.

Sharren goes outside with the dog in the backyard for quiet time for five or ten minute breaks if she needs to. Jacob watches Ari. He can open the back door and get Sharren if Arianna needs her.

As standup comics have said, the reason a lot of men (and women) stop at bars on the way home is so they can decompress before coming home to the chaos that is at home. I look forward to coming home because I have a routine that helps me unwind:

1. Enter the house.
2. Hugs and kisses for everybody.
3. Check my mail and e-mail.
4. Listen to what everybody did for the day.
5. Try to meditate or at least relax by myself before dinner.

If I am very tired I try to relax before entering the house by meditating (and it can be nothing more than relaxing and just closing your eyes and breathing in and out slowly letting go of your thoughts for a few minutes). Just park your car somewhere safe so you don' get ticketed or towed and relax if you need to.

This is very important when you are wrapped up in something super-emotional like receiving a diagnosis that your daughter has Rett's Syndrome (or frankly, any diagnosis like that).

The reason I also go straight home to my family after work is because experience has shown me that there are a lot of issues that need to be addressed ("the fridge/car/computer isn't working"), items that need to be recognized ("I got an A on my midterm") and feelings of being missed that need to be acknowledged with hugs and kisses!

If you are the type of person who needs his or her quiet time – by all means let your family know and give yourself fifteen minutes to half an hour. If there is something pressing that has to be taken care of I explain to my family what I am doing and I take the brief time to resolve whatever it is. As long as you are communicating and you do follow through immediately by returning to your family time, they should understand and you should have minimum problems.

If you are a single parent – you may want to go somewhere other than home to decompress depending on how many children are at home waiting for you, etc.

Sorry for digressing on how I deal with anger or stress but I figured it might help.

Here are some sobering figures about Rett's Syndrome:

Rett's Syndrome can happen to one out of fifteen thousand females. That is pretty common when you take a look at the size of the United States, the continent and then the world.

In the United States, in 2005, the female population was roughly 150,425,351 that means there were 10,029 Rett's Syndrome girls.

The female population of the United Kingdom in 2005 was about 30,558,236 people give or take. That means that there were about 2,038 Rett's Syndrome girls – most of them not diagnosed correctly.

Carrying this out logically, the world female population in 2005 was roughly 3,200,960,398 people. That means that there are around 213,397 Rett's girls out on the planet!

This does not take into account undocumented people who avoid census takers!

In general, according to the U.S. Department of Health and Human Services, there are approximately 9 million children who require special needs care in the United States. That makes it one in five households is caring for a special needs child.

Returning to my "not" items – it goes without saying that the following is true:

It is NOT a punishment from God.

There, I said it. What is God going to do, give me a child with Rett's Syndrome? Too late, my wife and I did that on our own already.

In all seriousness, these feelings come from the fear and guilt reaction. Fear is a normal reaction but again, with understanding the diagnosis you can sort fact from fiction. In our case, our imaginations expected the worse from a bad situation.

It is normal to be worried about your future, your daughter's future, medical care, costs, what will happen to the child at certain ages, etc.

It is also interesting to note that our first "go to" reaction is that God or the universe is out to get us. If we break it down, isn't it pretty selfish of us to think that God, being All Mighty is out to get us specifically for something we did or did not do?

When we think about this logically though, it doesn't make sense – from a religious or scientific perspective.

If you were raised to believe in God, the foremost thing in all religions is that God is love and He (or She) believes in Compassion and Mercy.

Mutated genes on the other hand, are ignorant of God and only do what they are molecular built to do, namely, mutate and they could care less whether you believe in God, evolution or that the universe was created by a guy named Fred in 1937.

Rett's Syndrome affects people ALL over the world regardless of their race, creed, color, religion or financial status. Think I am joking? Take a look at some of the Rett groups I will talk about later and see for yourself.

What makes you or I so special that God would single us out to give our daughters Rett's Syndrome?

My favorite answer to people who try to, if I can use the 1960's hippy culture expression, "lay a trip on you" is that, "Actually, God gave us a Rett girl (please feel free to insert any other special needs child here) because He (or She) knew that we would take care of her."

If I am feeling extra petty, I will add, "See? God loves us more than you! Ha ha ha ha!"

I was just kidding about that last sentence.

Which leads me to my next "not" statement.....

It is NOT because you may have made jokes about disabled people when you were younger.

If that were the case, a lot of really rotten people would get what is coming to them but as we all know, the real world doesn't work that way.

Your sense of humor will grow substantially in caring for a Rett's girl (or any other special needs person for that matter) because you begin to gain insight. You may have had insight before it is nothing like what you will start to witness with your child and the world around you.

Ancient mystics in Aramaic use to call insight "Kashf". You will start developing through observation with your daughter deeper understanding of human personalities, communication and as a result of that your sense of humor will grow.

How does that work? Things that you use to consider important will no longer be an issue. For example, when Arianna would start to squawk while walking in a mall, she would be trying to communicate with somebody. At first, I would feel some slight self consciousness about Arianna but if people start to stare or gawk you will realize that it is their problem, not your daughters and not yours!

It is NOT because your mother said, "Wait till you have kids of your own someday!"

As much as we all would love to blame somebody else, sorry, our moms are off the hook on this one...

By the same token, do NOT let your parents, relatives or friends start pointing the finger at you that it was your fault. That is insensitive and ignorant.

If they choose, like a lot of people to distance themselves from you out of fear, ignorance or what have you, that is there choice.

Try to educate them.

Buy them a copy of this book!!!!

Take your daughter over and show that Rett Syndrome is not contagious!!!

If they still run away – throw your hands in the air and ask God, Buddha or the Universe to watch over them and let them go. You don't need them in your life anyways because you have your hands full. You also have an angel to take care of.

It is NOT because you ate pork.

At least until scientific evidence comes up to the contrary. Seriously, it is not because you ate pork or broke any "religious" rite. Genes cannot see what you put in your mouth.

It is okay that you also are experiencing a lot of deep feelings.

In fact, you may be overwhelmed by feelings of confusion, a sense of weakness – powerlessness, and even anger towards your daughter.

If the feelings are overwhelming – please seek professional help in the form of social services, doctors, or understanding clergy members. Put down the book and do it NOW!

No matter how bleak and dismal you are feeling – YOU ARE NOT ALONE! YOU WILL GET THROUGH THIS!

Come back when you are feeling better and continue with the book.

Take comfort in knowing that you are not alone and that every parent who has had a special needs child goes through some or even all of those emotions.

Now what are some of the things that this is:

It IS an opportunity to learn how much you can deal with life.

It IS a chance to help your daughter with a situation that is frightening and unknown. Can you imagine if you were starting to develop the ability to speak and have it

taken away? Or watched as your body
failed to respond to your desires?

Your daughter will need all the love and
understanding you can muster!
It IS an opportunity to remember that if you
have other children and a spouse that they
need love and you ALL have to work
together as a family.

"Normal" siblings need to be told that if
they need extra attention they should ask
for it. When they ask for it, give it to them.
They are pretty overwhelmed themselves
and they need you to tell them that their
sister needs some extra help because she is
different not because you love them any
more or less.

Plan special independent days for doing
things with your healthy children by
themselves as well as a family. For
example, Jacob my son and I go to sporting
events, movies and places without Sharren
and Arianna. We've also gone camping in
scouts. Make as much of a normal life that
you can with your children.

It IS an opportunity to clear out all the nonsense in your life and start worrying about important things and relaxing about little things.

It IS the time to become self-realized! What does that mean? It means you can choose to stop worrying about what people think about you and your daughter. You will get a lot of stares from ignorant people in the supermarket. Stupid adults and children might start staring and whispering sometimes when you walk by.

Who cares?

You will be devoting your energy to important things and life and not worrying about what others think. You will realize what is important in your life.

CHAPTER TWO

ARIANNA'S STORY

Arianna was born Oct 14, 1996. She was a great little girl who screamed and did not sleep through the night. When Arianna came home from the hospital, she started exhibiting normal curiosity about things all around her.

She did not crawl as she developed but rather rolled. She did learn to walk though her gait was stiff. She also had mastered some basic words like "Dad" "Mom" "Yes" "No" and a few others.

Whenever the family would be in the living room getting ready to watch a movie on tv, Sharren or I would make popcorn and Arianna would say "popcorn".

Around one to one and a half years old Arianna started exhibiting what is commonly called "Night Terrors". She would wake up with blood curdling screams and she would be crying. Sharren and I thought at first it was just nightmares. Then I thought inter-dimensional beings were attacking Arianna. Then Sharren told me to stop watching so much science fiction before bed...I am just kidding about the last two sentences. Really!

Our son Jacob would wake up as well from the noise and we would all try to go back to sleep.

It was one of the most frightening things a parent can go through and believe me, Sharren and I went through some pretty frightening things. If your daughter is going through this phase (and again some girls don't), it is "normal" and try to comfort your girl as best as possible.

Arianna use to walk around the house and all of a sudden she started wind-milling her arms. She would also start pulling her hair out and putting it in her mouth. Sharren and I would first ask her politely to stop it and then as parents do, figure raising our voices would work (it didn't so we stopped that).

Arianna would come over to us and try to say something but the words would not come out. I would look into her eyes and see the frustration as she was trying to communicate something and I would start asking her if she wanted something to eat, drink, change her movie on the dvd player, anything.

I would bring popcorn in a bowl over to her and ask her "Can you say 'popcorn' or even 'pop'? " She sometimes would after several minutes and then she stopped saying it entirely. She would have a look of utter frustration on her face, windmill her arms and scream.

We turned to a speech therapist at first to see if there was something wrong with Arianna's speech – the therapist couldn't help. She and our physician thought it might be autism and we went to a specialist in Beverly Hills who saw Arianna, gave her some tests and diagnosed her with Rett's Syndrome.

Unfortunately, the information she handed us was from several decades ago and there was a note in there about prognosis being early death and we were very depressed.

One good thing was that the genetic blood test to see if there was Rett's Syndrome was out and we were planning on having Arianna's blood tested for Rett's.

I researched on the internet and found a lot of information on Rett's Syndrome and more recent research and surveys. Things were not as bleak as they were presented to us.

We learned about the various Rett support and research groups – you will too.

We also spend a lot of time and attention with Jacob, Arianna's older brother. He loves his younger sister, is very protective and a great human being.

Arianna communicates to us with her eyes, and by walking over to us when she wants something. In the case of Arianna and for some Rett's girls, it is about context. If Arianna has been watching a video or dvd in her room and she walks over, the chances are that the movie is over and she wants another one. If it is close to dinner time, she will come over and sometimes she will sign "eat".

Sometimes she will need a change of diapers, sometimes she just wants to see what is going on and see what tv shows we are watching. Arianna likes some cartoons including the Simpsons and Family Guy.

Rett's girls have sparkling eyes and are good listeners. Ari is no exception unless she is tired in which case she lets you know it.

Depth perception is an issue because Arianna sometimes will not walk up or down steps.
We take her hand and help her down the stairs and up the stairs. Sometimes she plays games and decides she wants to be

carried. Hey, sometimes I want to be carried up and down stairs too!

Discover the details with your daughter and start taking pictures, making notes, etc. because it will lead to a greater understanding through observation and in turn make you not only a better parent for taking care of your child (by the way, congratulations, you ARE a great parent!) but a better student of life because you can observe things in better detail.

Remember the more insight you develop, the more insight you can share with your daughter, your family and the world.

CHAPTER THREE

SEIZURES

Our number one issue with Arianna is her seizures. Arianna would get seizures where she would freeze up and stop moving. If she were standing, she would fall or try to catch herself. We went through a lot of anti-seizure medicines to see what would work and what wouldn't.

Common problems that we encountered with anti-seizure medicines for us were trying to get Arianna to take it – we had to disguise it at times in her food. If the dosage was too strong, Arianna would be too sleepy.

Arianna goes to school and she would sleep on the bus sometimes and sometimes during class. It would be a drag because she would sleep through activities and therapy. Ugh.

Maybe you are going through this too. If so, talk with other Rett's parents to see what worked for them – it may work for your daughter.

You may find that for your daughter that some medicines work and some don't. You will also want to watch the side effects and remember that the name of the game is to improve the quality of your daughter's life!

My wife and I opted for one solution called a Vagus Nerve Stimulator (also known by its acronym "VNS").

The VNS is a generator that sends electrical stimulation to the brain through the vagus nerve. The surgical procedure was done in a few hours and Ari was able to leave the hospital after a few hours when she woke up.

It is not for everybody, and you should consult your physician, but so far, it has minimized the seizures that Arianna has been suffering. Arianna also has been trying to communicate more. She has started saying "hi" again in appropriate settings if somebody is talking to her. That is a big deal for my wife and I because that means that we can continue to work on getting her to communicate more.

She is more awake and responsive than she was before. The settings on the VNS can be adjusted to deliver different electrical stimulation time frames. A good doctor will also gradually adjust the settings and eventually try to wean your daughter off of any anti-seizure medicines that she is on. We are in the stage where we are starting to wean Arianna off of her meds – or as much as we can.

CHAPTER FOUR

WALKING

Walking is VERY important if your daughter is able to walk. Keep her moving. Keep her exercising.

Even if your daughter cannot walk, it is important that you keep her flexible. One of the more serious problems for Rett girls is their spines curving.   Helping the girls bend and relax is one way to try to keep them from surgery later on.

Equestrian therapy, having Arianna ride a horse and then perform light jousting and other activities while on the horse has helped Arianna with her sense of balance and walking. We have noted that the weeks that we miss the therapy she tends to wobble a little more rather than walk straight.

The Institute of Equestrian Therapy has been a blessing because it has kept Arianna mobile. Our special thanks goes out to Jacques Fouchaux, the director, for doing a wonderful job with Arianna as well as the other special needs children that are receiving therapy! Jacques was the founder of equestrian therapy and brought it to the United States in the 1960s.

Sharren and I have Arianna walk as much as possible. We keep her special needs stroller nearby but whenever we can let Arianna walk. Even if your daughters do not walk – please consult with your doctor and a physical therapist and take the time to exercise their muscles and gently stretch them.

It will help them as they get older and hopefully prevent problems which may develop with their backs!

CHAPTER FIVE

COMMUNICATION

One of the most frustrating things is trying to communicate with your daughter. I am going to go into some of the tools that we have tried with Arianna.

BIG BUTTONS
Big Buttons are basically two giant plastic button switches that are connected to a battery and a computer chip that has recorded on it different words. Common ones are "yes" and "no" and they correspond to the same words written (or taped) to the buttons. Each button is generally a different color (for example, one is red and the other is green) and the purpose is to get your daughter to communicate touching the button.

We tried one of these with Ari and she only uses the device sporadically. Part of the reason is for Rett Syndrome, she may not be as in control of her hand that particular day and it requires her to at least slap the button to make it work. That may be too much work for her.

PECS (Picture Exchange Communication System)

The PECS system consists of pictures with the word associated with it underneath and either taped on the wall, in a tray, etc and similar to the big buttons, the girl needs to point or touch the item that she wants. The difference between PECS and the Big Buttons is that PECS is used for multiple choices rather than yes/no choices. I suppose one can get more buttons and record the actions or choices on them but the buttons are more expensive than making paper or plastic pictures with print.

Arianna uses PECS sometimes when she is hungry. We have a PEC card for eat and she sometimes uses that. Arianna's school is starting as of December 2005, a program to get Arianna back responding to PECS.

SIGN LANGUAGE

Arianna started to learn Universal sign language at school a few years ago. She can sign "eat" and "more" and can sometimes sign what she wants. That is only when she is very, very hungry though. Because she has no purposeful use of her hands at times, she has a hard time signing. Arianna's school is not supporting sign language at this time.

CHAPTER SIX

FAMILY SANITY

The number one thing that you should worry about after your daughter is the sanity and health of you and your family. Ways to cope with being a Rett parent (or any other kind of special needs parent) is to network with other Rett's Syndrome parents, routine, and communication.

Rett girls love routine – in fact, for a lot of special needs individuals, routine is comfort for them. That is good and bad. The good news is that it can simplify things and provide solace for you and your family because when you do something over and over again, like a clock, you get very good at it. You will draw strength from it.

The bad news about routines is that they are boring and you would like to broaden your horizons as well as your daughters and other family members.

For Arianna, her routine consists of waking up, watching television, getting ready for school, breakfast, and then school. When she comes home, it's interaction with the family, television and dinner and socialization before bedtime. This is great because it gives Ari a basis for growing in a safe environment.

We try to plan outings, parties, etc so that Arianna can take things in small doses till she gets use to something. One example for us was going to the movies. When Arianna gets bored with a movie she starts getting restless and wants to walk around. If Arianna cannot walk around, she starts to squawk. When we go the movies as a family, we sometimes let Arianna walk around a lot before entering the theater. There have been many times though that Sharren has had to wait in the lobby with Arianna or I will tag team with her so we don't disrupt the movies for others. Arianna though has been getting better about sitting through a movie as she has been getting older. Not unlike normal child development, huh?

Ari loves to flirt with guys with her eyes and by smiling. If she is in an uncomfortable situation or in a crowd that is too loud, she gets agitated. Sharren or I try to hold her or at the very least put our hands on Ari if she is uncomfortable. Again, as she is getting older, she is getting better with public activities.

I strongly urge all parents to take their children and their siblings to ball games, movies, picnic events, anything that helps keep you connected to the community and allow you to socialize in what is perceived as "normal fun". You will find that helps tremendously in keeping your head and your family's head together.

Try to get season passes (if you can afford it) for amusement parks if your daughter responds well to them. Ari loves Disneyland and Universal Studios here in Southern California and she has a good time generally when we go there. There is usually good access for special needs (i.e., for wheelchairs or chair strollers) and generally the staff is helpful.

We don't have passes for Disneyland. We are not close enough to make it worth our while to go often enough so we go there only once or twice a year. They have also gotten expensive over the years.

For us, Universal Studios is closer and they usually have rolling special offers that we take advantage of for memberships. Until the price of gasoline gets lower, we try to limit our longer distance trips.

If you live in a climate such as the Midwest or Northeastern United States or another country that gets snowed in – look for recreational centers or organizations that have indoor gyms, malls, or swimming pools.

Always make sure that when you are planning a day trip or will be in your vehicle for extended periods of time that you have enough food for snacks for your family and enough medicine if you need it for your daughter. That is common sense but you would be surprised at how many people forget. It can mean the difference between keeping your sanity or losing it on a family outing.

While we are on the subject of travel – make sure you have enough diapers and baby wipes. Arianna as of this edition of the book is not toilet trained and we always keep some spares in either the car or her backpack. Finding a suitable spot to change her is another story but you always want to try to find somewhere where you have some elbow room. If you own a van, you can always use the van if you can make some free space inside of it.

Here is a tip: Most amusement park first aid stations have full size beds where you can change diapers on when your child is too big for changing tables. They have no problem letting you use them.

Jacob and I get away at least once a week for "guy stuff". That means we either go to a movie, sporting event, or shopping by ourselves. This way I get to bond with him and he gets one-on-one attention. It gives us a chance to go out, hang out, get into fights with one another, make-up, and rob a liquor store or two.

The last sentence was just to see if you were paying attention. Just kidding.

One of the biggest things that Sharren and I try to do is recharge our batteries. Whether that is each of us getting some private time or going out without any children around. Don't kid yourself. It can be very draining providing the support and care for a Rett's girl or any other special needs child. You owe it to yourself to insure that you are able to relax and recharge your batteries. You can love them and take care of them a lot better when you are healthy yourself.

If you are a single caregiver, take the time to try to meditate. Sit quietly as we discussed a little earlier. Clear your head and relax. If you need to sleep, sleep.

It is very easy to also fall into a diet of junk food. Please be very careful and wary of this. It is expensive and time consuming at times to provide healthy food and fast food is a quick and dirty solution for feeding the family. All I am asking is to try and not make a habit of it. There are a lot of fresh and inexpensive frozen foods at the supermarket. That being said, when we are running around it is not unusual to live on fast food for two or three days. We try really hard though not to fall into that trap.

As of this edition of the book we have a cat and a dog. Pisicu, our cat (pronounced "p-seek-ahhh", the name in Rumanian means "cat" by the way) is an orca colored (black and white colored) cat. Shiloh, our dog, is part retriever, part shepherd and chow.

Arianna has been okay with the animals and both the dog and cat are very gentle when they hang around Arianna. Shiloh had actually tried to get underneath Arianna when she was having a seizure once (rumor was she was partially trained as a special needs aid dog but that doesn't seem to be the case all the time). Both animals love to hang around Arianna when she is eating for scraps. Actually, they hang around anybody in the house who is eating. They are more like pigs than cat or dog. If you have the time and energy to take care of pets and you are cool with sanitation and keeping the house clean, I encourage you to have pets. If they are another thing you have to worry about (and we might get to that point as the animals get older) then don't get any animals. It goes without saying that if your daughter generally dislikes animals or anybody has allergies to keep them away as well.

You will need to find the one thing that you need to keep your life balanced. Everybody needs time to themselves, or alone with their spouse, boyfriend, girl friend, etc. It is not easy. If you have a support system of relatives – great! That is wonderful and more power to you. If you don't, you need to make do with what you have and try to get something that will work for you.

If you find and get a good, honest, safe babysitter they are worth their weight in gold. Places to look are colleges, high schools and of course, references from other parents with or without special needs children. For California, the sitter will need to know CPR and for most people of any age, certification can generally be done in a day or two.

Have the sitter spend some time with your daughter while you are around. Watch both the sitter and your daughter's reaction. Show the sitter your daughter's routine. If you are paranoid make sure the nanny camera is hidden and up and running....

When Sharren and I first started going out without the kids we spent most of the evening worrying about them. Eventually you should hit a comfort and trust zone where you will actually be able to go out and relax and have a good time.

Keeping our backs in good shape is very important to Sharren and me. When Arianna is tired and does not want to move, she does not move. End of story. When you are lifting basically a dead weight you need to be in good shape. Remember as you get older this won't get any easier. Sharren and I try to do at least basic stretching every day to stay healthy.

If you are unable to lift your daughter, please look into getting some mechanical aid with special needs lifts, etc.

Depending on what state you live in, you should contact the various state or county social service agencies to see what programs they have that might help you. With just a diagnosis of autism you will probably get more aid then if it were a Rett Syndrome diagnosis. That is because Rett's is not a mainstream disease. Please start writing your congressmen, city council people and anybody who has a say in setting up funding for special needs to call their attention to this disease.

Send them pictures of your daughter. By putting a personal face on the issue they will see that this is something that is happening here and now. At the time of the printing of this book, a lot of money is going into rebuilding the southern United States from being hit by Hurricane Katrina. A lot of money is going to Asia for earthquake relief. We need to make sure that WE get heard otherwise it will get harder and harder than it already is to try to get funding for our girls.

You can find (as of November 2005) your representative through here:

http://www.congressmerge.com/

One of the hardest things to do is start planning for what to do after you as a parent are no longer around. Start thinking about what kind of arrangements and services you would need to have in places for your daughter to have a safe, nurturing environment. If you are like most people, it is hard to save money.

Some sobering information is that it would take anywhere between $2,000,000 to $5,000,000 in a savings account yielding between 7 and 3% annual return of interest to cover annual expenses so that the principal would never have to be touched.

Try to start saving at least something. Compound interest is a very mighty tool that can help or hurt you. If you are saving over time, it can help you as your savings grow. If you are paying credit card interest, it will hurt you.

If you are in debt, do what you can to start climbing out. There have been recent changes in bankruptcy laws and you still may be able to work things out with creditors. If you don't own a home and your situation is that owning a home would be a good thing for you, start saving money and get ready for a lot of real estate foreclosures that will be happening soon once the people who have variable rate loans start having their monthly payments go up.

As of the writing of this edition of the book, the current government here in the United States is looking at changing and simplifying tax law. One of the items up for discussion is the mortgage interest deduction. Personally, I don't think Congress will get rid of it but it is a good idea to keep current of what is going on with tax laws. Ultimately, that will affect you and your family regardless if there is a special needs child in your home or not. (Note: As an addendum – President Bush has tabled the proposals for simplifying tax law as of December 2005).

Do some research and if need be, consult with some financial experts but remember that the so-called experts are human beings and that ultimately the decision for investing and saving rests with you. Talk with other special needs parents as well to see what they have set up and going on.

If you live in a state that has programs for aid at the age of 18 or 21, make sure that you start filling out the appropriate forms early enough so you can qualify your daughter so she can start receiving benefits and services.

It is important that I mention also that you need to know what your employer is like before you can comfortably discuss your daughter's condition. Some employers will balk and freak out at keeping you (or hiring you) because of the potential medical costs they perceive they will have to cover for your daughter. Others will step up to the plate and be helpful and sensitive. Only you can judge how much you want to tell an employer.

There are many fine resources on the internet as stated earlier that get into detail with specific situations about Rett's Syndrome. Some are mentioned at the end of the book.

Here is something that generally is not covered.

If you are a single parent, you are going through a very tough time and the chances are you want to curl up into a corner and vegetate.

Don't.

Or at least if you do, make it for short periods to recharge your batteries and then get on with life.
You can and will be a social butterfly again. You will be able to date and meet people at the very least start socializing with other Rett families and with people in general. I cannot promise you that you will find a great husband, wife or partner but you will not know unless you try. So, please, don't

give up on your social life just because of
Rett's Syndrome. Just use common sense
and remember that you want people you
can trust to be around you and your
daughter.

MENSTRUATION

One of the things that will happen is that
your girl will develop to a certain degree
physically into womanhood as any other
girl will. You may want to talk to other Rett
parents who have had a daughter go
through puberty to discuss safe, chemical
methods of stopping her period.

I don't have anything to add to this
personally at this time because our
daughter has not hit puberty. It will be
covered more in depth in subsequent
editions of this book.

IN CLOSING

I hope this book helped you in some way.

There are many issues that I have not had to deal with yet and as I do, I will cover them in expanded editions of this book.

I wish you and your loved ones as Benjamin Franklin said, "To Be Healthy, Wealthy and Wise" and I would like to add "Happy".

You will make it. I know it!

CHAPTER SEVEN

ARIANNA'S DEVELOPMENT INFORMATION

Arianna was born October 14, 1996. She was 6 pounds and 15 ounces. She was 19 inches long. She came home from the hospital with us when she was 12 hours old.

Arianna as a baby was very good but she did not sleep well. She would not take a pacifier or a bottle. Sharren decided to move to the family room to sleep with Arianna because her screaming was keeping Jacob up at night. Ari was not sleeping more than a half an hour at a time and she was hungry all the time. Ari would sleep in a swing for half an hour, wake up, eat and throw up then go back to sleep. She managed to gain 2 ½ pounds by her 3 week check up.

At 1 ½ months, Arianna found her thumb and started sucking on that between meals.

At her 2 month check up she gained another 2 pounds. At four months she gained 3 pounds.

Even though Arianna had gained an additional 2 pounds at her 6 month check-up, the doctor was worried because Ari could not sit up yet. During this time, Arianna would look at toys but never try to play with them. One of the toys, a gym play set we would place Ari under. She wouldn't do a thing with it. When we would hit the toy she would laugh but she wouldn't hit it on her own.

At this time, her bottom teeth came in and she still liked to eat every half hour. We experimented with several different baby bottles over six months till we found one that Arianna liked.

At nine months, Arianna had gained another 2 pounds and was sitting up. The doctor noted that Arianna rolled around and did not do any crawling. Ari use to roll all around the house instead of crawl.

At this age, she would sleep for three hours at a time (usually 8 PM – 11 PM) and then take 10 minute catnaps the rest of the night.

Sharren found out that Arianna liked to be placed in a semi-upright position in a bean bag chair and she would be quiet and watch videos. That gave her a break and helped Sharren sleep more at night.

At Arianna's one year check up, she gained another 2 pounds but the doctor mentioned that Ari's head did not grow very much.

Arianna continued to roll and was not trying to walk or pull herself up. We bought her a walker but she could not make it move. We stood her up and tried putting one foot in front of another. We kept this up for two months till Ari was fourteen months old. She was able to stand up without any assistance but she still needed something to hold onto to walk.

At fifteen months she gained still another 2 pounds and her head was 18 inches. The doctor was happy. We were happy that Ari could also go for two hours between meals because she was on more solid foods.

At eighteen months Arianna had gained 5 more pounds but her head did not grow. He said Ari should be talking more and we should work with her. Sharren and I did.

At two years we were sent to a speech pathologist because Arianna had lost her speech. She was walking with assistance and he had stopped measuring her head.

Two months short of her third birthday, Arianna was able to walk without assistance. That was a huge milestone for all of us!

The speech pathologist sent us to a developmental pediatric specialist. Ari was not talking at all now. She observed Arianna moving her eyes side to side and then rolling them. Later on, we found out these were seizures. Arianna had a wide based gait and poor trunk rotation.

We were told that Arianna's muscle tone
was hypotinic. When trying to get Ari to
engage in activities such as using a slide or
riding a tricycle, she did not seem to have
any idea of what to do with her feet. We
would have to show her and move her feet
for her. Arianna would also climb onto a
sofa using her legs and not her arms or
hands.

She would hold her arms behind her and
lean back. Arianna would roll on her back
at this time and would zone out to what
was going on around her. She would start
making a teepee with her fingers.

When Arianna was three and we received
the preliminary Rett Syndrome diagnosis
we also were told Ari should get an EEG. I
already mentioned how devastated Sharren
and I were due to the fact the paperwork we
had was very old. We researched on the
internet for more current information.

Ari had an EEG done in December 1999
and we found out she was having seizures.

Ari was placed on Depakote for her seizures.

At three and a half, Arianna started a special needs pre-school. We started paying very close attention to Ari's reactions to the school. We were looking at another school in the neighborhood as well. Arianna cried the whole time we were at the first school. At the second school she was happy and walking around checking everything out.

Occupational therapy helped and Ari was showing great progress until she was 5. We were told it was up to the school to continue with the therapy. We did not get it as frequently as we did before.

In April 2000 we received back the results of Arianna's blood test for Rett's Syndrome. It came back with the interpretation that she had the mutation in exon 3 of the MECP2 gene. The mutation confirms the diagnosis of Rett Syndrome.

Arianna was pulling her hair and mouthing anything she could get her hands on. She was biting, pinching and pulling other people's hair. A pediatric neurologist measured her head and it was still 18 inches at 4 years old.

He placed her on a small dose of Prozac. After three days of taking it, her pinching, biting etc stopped and Ari started wringing her hands in the more "traditional" way of Rett Syndrome girls.

In November 2001, the neurologist found that Arianna also had a form of cerebral palsy and that was confirmed by a second neurologist. She had another EEG showing that she was still having seizures. Arianna was put on Tegretol.

At Arianna's five year check up In October 2001 the doctor was mad that Arianna had occupational therapy taken away and wrote a letter to her school for four times a week. Arianna gets therapy only one time a week now. Arianna was walking on her tip toes and an orthopedic surgeon ordered some ankle foot orthos (AFOs). The doctor also said that Ari had a 5% curvature of her spine. Arianna went to Equestrian Therapy and after a year her spine was straighter and she was walking better. Five years later, Ari has no curvature.

Our neurologist at the time closed his practice for health reasons. We found a new one and we had to try other anti-seizure medicines because the Tegretol did not seem to be working anymore.

In the summer of 2005, Arianna was having more seizures and for her age and weight it would have been harder to monitor the doses. Her neurologist had given us a packet on VNS. We talked to other parents who had gone through the procedure. We went ahead with it.

Arianna has had her head grow and she has gained weight since she had the VNS installed. It is also on a very low setting.

The procedure was straightforward.

She has had perhaps one or two small seizures since she had the VNS. When we changed the setting of the VNS, she had discomfort and we ended up lowering the setting back down.

At age 6, Arianna lost the ability to finger feed herself. She can still pick up a sippy cup, bring it to her mouth and drink with it. She cannot put it down. She drops the cup.

Arianna to this day still grinds her teeth. She does breath holding and swallowing air but only while she is awake. She eats well but she is also on PediaSure to help with weight gain.

It looks like Arianna is in "stage III". Her behavior is much better, she is less irritable, and she has a better attention span as well as better communication.

CHAPTER EIGHT

FLIP BOOK

I love flipbooks. I thought it would be cool
to have one here.

If you want to see the flip book, please flip
the pages quickly.

Y

YO

YOU

YOU R

YOU RO

YOU ROC

YOU ROCK

YOU ROCK!

CHAPTER NINE

MORE RETT SYNDROME INFO

The following information is from the public domain from the National Institute of Neurological Disorders and Stroke (NINDS) on Rett's Syndrome.

What is Rett syndrome?

Rett syndrome is a childhood neurodevelopmental disorder characterized by normal early development followed by loss of purposeful use of the hands, distinctive hand movements, slowed brain and head growth, gait abnormalities, seizures, and mental retardation. It affects females almost exclusively.
The disorder was identified by Dr. Andreas Rett, an Austrian physician who first described it in a journal article in 1966. It was not until after a second article about

the disorder was published in 1983 that the disorder was generally recognized.

The course of Rett syndrome, including the age of onset and the severity of symptoms, varies from child to child. Before the symptoms begin, however, the child appears to grow and develop normally. Then, gradually, mental and physical symptoms appear. Hypotonia (loss of muscle tone) is usually the first symptom. As the syndrome progresses, the child loses purposeful use of her hands and the ability to speak. Other early symptoms may include problems crawling or walking and diminished eye contact. The loss of functional use of the hands is followed by compulsive hand movements such as wringing and washing. The onset of this period of regression is sometimes sudden. Another symptom, apraxia — the inability to perform motor functions — is perhaps the most severely disabling feature of Rett syndrome, interfering with every body movement, including eye gaze and speech. Individuals with Rett syndrome often exhibit autistic-like behaviors in the early stages. Other symptoms may include toe walking; sleep problems; wide-based gait; teeth grinding and difficulty chewing; slowed growth; seizures; cognitive disabilities; and breathing difficulties while awake such as hyperventilation, apnea (breath holding), and air swallowing.

What are the stages of the disorder?

There are four stages of Rett syndrome. Stage I, called *early onset,* generally begins between 6 and 18 months of age. Quite frequently, this stage is overlooked because symptoms of the disorder may be somewhat vague, and parents and doctors may not notice the subtle slowing of development at first. The infant may begin to show less eye contact and have reduced interest in toys. There may be delays in gross motor skills such as sitting or crawling. Hand-wringing and decreasing head growth may occur, but not enough to draw attention. This stage usually lasts for a few months but can persist for more than a year.

Stage II, or the **rapid destructive** stage, usually begins between ages 1 and 4 and may last for weeks or months. This stage may have either a rapid or a gradual onset as purposeful hand skills and spoken language are lost. The characteristic hand movements begin to emerge during this stage and often include wringing, washing, clapping, or tapping, as well as repeatedly moving the hands to the mouth. Hands are sometimes clasped behind the back or held at the sides, with random touching, grasping, and releasing. The movements persist while the child is awake but disappear during sleep. Breathing irregularities such as episodes of apnea and hyperventilation may occur, although breathing is usually normal during sleep. Some girls also display autistic-like symptoms such as loss of social interaction and communication. General irritability and sleep irregularities may be seen. Gait patterns are unsteady and initiating motor movements can be difficult. Slowing of head growth is usually noticed during this stage. Stage III, also called the **plateau** or **pseudo-stationary** stage, usually begins between ages 2 and 10 and can last for years. Apraxia, motor problems, and seizures are prominent during this stage. However, there may be improvement in behavior, with less irritability, crying, and autistic-like features. An individual in stage III may show more interest in her surroundings, and her alertness, attention span, and communication skills may improve. Many girls remain in this stage for most of their lives.

The last stage, stage IV — called the **late motor deterioration** stage — can last for years or decades and is characterized by reduced mobility. Muscle weakness, rigidity (stiffness), spasticity, dystonia (increased muscle tone with abnormal posturing of extremity or trunk), and scoliosis (curvature of the spine) are other prominent features. Girls who were previously able to walk may stop walking. Generally, there is no decline in cognition, communication, or hand skills in stage IV. Repetitive hand movements may decrease, and eye gaze usually improves.

What causes Rett syndrome?

Rett syndrome is caused by mutations (structural alterations or defects) in the MECP2 (pronounced *meck-pea-two*) gene, which is found on the X chromosome (*see* section on "Who gets Rett syndrome" for a discussion of the importance of the involvement of the X chromosome). Scientists identified the gene — which is believed to control the functions of several other genes — in 1999. The MECP2 gene contains instructions for the synthesis of a protein called methyl cytosine binding protein 2 (MeCP2), which acts as one of the many biochemical switches that tell other genes when to turn off and stop producing their own unique proteins. Because the MECP2 gene does not function properly in those with Rett syndrome, insufficient amounts or structurally abnormal forms of the protein are formed. The absence or malfunction of the protein is thought to cause other genes to be abnormally expressed, but this hypothesis has not yet been confirmed.

Seventy to 80 percent of girls given a diagnosis of Rett syndrome have the MECP2 genetic mutation detected by current diagnostic techniques. Scientists believe the remaining 20 to 30 percent of cases may be caused by partial gene deletions, by mutations in other parts of the gene, or by genes that have not yet been identified; thus, they continue to search for other mutations.

Is Rett syndrome inherited?

Although Rett syndrome is a genetic disorder — resulting from a faulty gene or genes — less than 1 percent of recorded cases are inherited or passed from one generation to the next. Most cases are sporadic, which means the mutation occurs randomly, mostly during spermatogenesis, and is not inherited.

Who gets Rett syndrome?

Rett syndrome affects one in every 10,000 to 15,000 live female births. It occurs in all racial and ethnic groups worldwide. Prenatal testing is available for families with an affected daughter who has an identified MECP2 mutation. Since the disorder occurs spontaneously in most affected individuals, however, the risk of a family having a second child with the disorder is less than 1 percent.

Genetic testing is also available for sisters of girls with Rett syndrome and an identified MECP2 mutation to determine if they are asymptomatic carriers of the disorder, which is an extremely rare possibility.

Girls have two X chromosomes, but only one is active in any given cell. This means that in a child with Rett syndrome only about half the cells in the nervous system will use the defective gene. Some of the child's brain cells use the healthy gene and express normal amounts of the proteins.

The story is different for boys who have an MECP2 mutation known to cause Rett syndrome in girls. Because boys have only one X chromosome they lack a back-up copy that could compensate for the defective one, and they have no protection from the harmful effects of the disorder. Boys with such a defect die shortly after birth.

Different types of mutations in the MECP2 gene can cause mental retardation in boys.

How is Rett syndrome diagnosed?

Doctors diagnose Rett syndrome by observing signs and symptoms during the child's early growth and development, and conducting ongoing evaluations of the child's physical and neurological status. Recently, scientists developed a genetic test to confirm the clinical diagnosis of this disorder; the test involves searching for the MECP2 mutation on the child's X chromosome. Given what we know about the genes involved in Rett syndrome, such tests are able to confirm a clinical diagnosis in up to 80 percent of all cases.

Some children who have Rett syndrome-like characteristics or MECP2 genetic mutations do not fulfill the diagnostic criteria for the syndrome as defined below. These persons are described as having "atypical" or "variant" Rett syndrome. Atypical cases account for about 15 percent of the total number of diagnosed cases.

A pediatric neurologist or developmental pediatrician should be consulted to confirm the clinical diagnosis of Rett syndrome. The physician will use a highly specific set of guidelines that are divided into three types of clinical criteria: **essential, supportive,** and **exclusion.** The presence of any of the exclusion criteria negates a diagnosis of "classic" or "typical" Rett syndrome.

Examples of **essential** diagnostic criteria or symptoms include having apparently normal development until between the ages of 6 and 18 months and having normal head circumference at birth followed by a slowing of the rate of head growth with age (between 3 months and 4 years). Other essential diagnostic criteria include severely

impaired expressive language, repetitive
hand movements, shaking of the torso, and
toe-walking or an unsteady, wide-based,
stiff-legged gait.

Supportive criteria are not required for a
diagnosis of Rett syndrome but may occur
in some patients. In addition, these
symptoms — which vary in severity from
child to child — may not be observed in
very young girls but may develop with age.
A child with supportive criteria but none of
the essential criteria does **not** have Rett
syndrome. Supportive criteria include
breathing difficulties; electroencephalogram
(EEG) abnormalities; seizures; muscle
rigidity, spasticity, and/or joint contracture
which worsen with age; scoliosis; teeth-
grinding; small feet in relation to height;
growth retardation; decreased body fat and
muscle mass (although there may be a
tendency toward obesity in some affected
adults); abnormal sleep patterns,
irritability, or agitation; chewing and/or
swallowing difficulties; poor circulation of
the lower extremities with cold and bluish-
red feet and legs; decreased mobility with
age; and constipation.

In addition to the essential diagnostic criteria, a number of specific conditions enable physicians to rule out a diagnosis of Rett syndrome. These are referred to as **exclusion** criteria. Children with any one of the following criteria do not have Rett syndrome: enlargement of body organs or other signs of storage disease, vision loss due to retinal disorder or optic atrophy, microcephaly at birth, an identifiable metabolic disorder or other inherited degenerative disorder, an acquired neurological disorder resulting from severe infection or head trauma, evidence of growth retardation in utero, or evidence of brain damage acquired after birth.

Why are some cases more severe than others?

The course and severity of Rett syndrome vary from individual to individual. Some girls have symptoms from birth onward, while others may have late regression or milder symptoms.

Because females have two copies of the X chromosome and need only one working copy for genetic information, they turn off the extra X chromosome in a process called *X inactivation.* This process occurs randomly so that each cell is left with one active X chromosome. The severity of Rett syndrome in girls is in part a function of the percentage of cells with a normal copy of the MECP2 gene after X inactivation takes place: if X inactivation turns off the X chromosome that is carrying the defective gene in a large proportion of cells, the symptoms will be mild, but if a larger percentage of cells have the X chromosome with the normal MECP2 gene turned off, onset of the disorder may occur earlier and the symptoms may be more severe.

Is treatment available?

There is no cure for Rett syndrome. Treatment for the disorder is symptomatic — focusing on the management of symptoms — and supportive, requiring a multidisciplinary approach. Medication may be needed for breathing irregularities and motor difficulties, and antiepileptic drugs may be used to control seizures. There should be regular monitoring for scoliosis and possible heart abnormalities. Occupational therapy (in which therapists help children develop skills needed for performing self-directed activities — *occupations* — such as dressing, feeding, and practicing arts and crafts), physiotherapy, and hydrotherapy may prolong mobility. Some children may require special equipment and aids such as braces to arrest scoliosis, splints to modify hand movements, and nutritional programs to help them maintain adequate weight. Special academic, social, vocational, and support services may also be required in some cases.

What is the outlook for those with Rett syndrome?

Despite the difficulties with symptoms, most individuals with Rett syndrome continue to live well into middle age and beyond. Because the disorder is rare, very little is known about long-term prognosis and life expectancy. While it is estimated that there are many middle-aged women (in their 40s and 50s) with the disorder, not enough women have been studied to make reliable estimates about life expectancy beyond age 40.

What research is being done?

Within the Federal Government, the National Institute of Neurological Disorders and Stroke (NINDS) and the National Institute of Child Health and Human Development (NICHD), two of the National Institutes of Health (NIH), support clinical and basic research on Rett syndrome. Understanding the cause of this disorder is necessary for developing new therapies to manage specific symptoms, as well as for providing better methods of diagnosis. The discovery of the Rett syndrome gene in 1999 provides a basis for further genetic studies and enables the use of recently developed animal models such as transgenic mice.

One NINDS-supported study is looking for mutations in the MECP2 gene of individuals with Rett syndrome to find out how the MeCP2 protein functions. Information from this study will increase understanding of the disorder and may lead to new therapies. Scientists know that lack of a properly functioning MeCP2 protein disturbs the function of mature brain cells but they do not know the exact mechanisms by which this happens. Investigators are also trying to find other genetic mutations that can cause Rett syndrome and other genetic switches that operate in a similar way to the MeCP2 protein. Once they discover how the protein works and locate similar switches, they may be able to devise therapies that can substitute for the malfunctioning switch. Another outcome might involve manipulating other biochemical pathways to compensate for the malfunctioning MECP2 gene, thus preventing progression of the disorder.

Where can I get more information?
For more information on neurological disorders or research programs funded by the National Institute of Neurological Disorders and Stroke, contact the Institute's Brain Resources and Information Network (BRAIN) at:
BRAIN
P.O. Box 5801
Bethesda, MD 20824
(800) 352-9424
www.ninds.nih.gov
Information also is available from the following organizations:
International Rett Syndrome Association (IRSA)
9121 Piscataway Road
Suite 2B
Clinton, MD   20735
irsa@rettsyndrome.org
http://www.rettsyndrome.org
Tel: 301-856-3334 800-818-RETT (7388)
Fax: 301-856-3336

Rett Syndrome Research Foundation (RSRF)
4600 Devitt Drive
Cincinnati, OH   45246
monica@rsrf.org
http://www.rsrf.org
Tel: 513-874-3020
Fax: 513-874-2520

National Institute of Child Health and Human Development (NICHD)
National Institutes of Health, DHHS
31 Center Drive, Rm. 2A32 MSC 2425
Bethesda, MD   20892-2425
http://www.nichd.nih.gov
Tel: 301-496-5133
Fax: 301-496-7101

National Institute of Child Health and Human Development (NICHD)
National Institutes of Health, DHHS
31 Center Drive, Rm. 2A32 MSC 2425
Bethesda, MD   20892-2425
http://www.nichd.nih.gov

Tel: 301-496-5133
Fax: 301-496-7101

Easter Seals
230 West Monroe Street
Suite 1800
Chicago, IL   60606-4802
info@easter-seals.org
http://www.easter-seals.org
Tel: 312-726-6200 800-221-6827
Fax: 312-726-1494

"Rett Syndrome Fact Sheet", NINDS.
NIH Publication No. 04-4863

Prepared by:
Office of Communications and Public
Liaison
National Institute of Neurological Disorders
and Stroke
National Institutes of Health
Bethesda, MD 20892

NINDS health-related material is provided for information purposes only and does not necessarily represent endorsement by or an official position of the National Institute of Neurological Disorders and Stroke or any other Federal agency. Advice on the treatment or care of an individual patient should be obtained through consultation with a physician who has examined that patient or is familiar with that patient's medical history.

CHAPTER TEN

COMMENTS ON REFERENCES AND ADDITIONAL RESOURCES:

http://www.rettsyndrome.org/

IRSA- The International Rett Syndrome Association. A good place to link up with the latest research and network with other Rett parents.

Kathy Hunter's book is the bible for Rett's Syndrome and the RettNet will hook you into real parents with the same issues that you have and they can tell you what works for them.
Take a few moments and join IRSA while you are at it. You will be glad you did! A portion from the sales of this book will be contributed to Rett research.

http://www.bcm.edu/pediatrics/index.cfm
?Realm=999911118&This_Template=pedi_ho
me.cfm

Baylor College's Blue Bird Rett Center is
another place to look for Rett information.

http://www.equestriantherapy.com/

If you are in the Southern California area
and have a special needs child please look
into the Equestrian Therapy that is offered
out here. It has done wonders for Arianna
and might do wonders for your child! If you
live out of the area, check local listings and
the internet to see if there is any equestrian
therapy near you.

INDEX

Printed in the United States
142985LV00001B/167/A

9 780977 728206